CODES

FOR

ENERGY

(Become your Authentic Self)

BY

MELVIS MICHAEL

COPYRIGHT © 2022 MELVIS MICHAEL
All rights reserved

Table of contents

Outline

Codes for Energy are a bunch of rules that
can assist you with accomplishing profound
arousing also, become your legitimate self. Melvis
Michael makes sense of how they work, what they
offer,
also, how to apply them in Codes for Energy
(2022). In the event that you as of now have the
essentials of
otherworldliness, and know your seven chakras, the
Codes will assist you with being much more on top
of them, as each Code relates to an alternate
chakra. Codes for Energy is intended to
capability as a solid extraordinary instrument that
depends on quantum material science, neuroscience,
and energy recuperating research. With Codes for
Energy, you might be something else entirely
form of yourself- - better, more joyful, and
more engaged in a couple of months, if
not weeks.

Chapter 1

Your True Potential

We all have encountered troubles that
have driven us to the place of weakness. Perhaps
you have an injured heart. Perhaps you've
been actually or genuinely unwell,
monetarily pushed, or disappointed. So many
things might cause us torment, including poor
confidence, hatred or lament, failure
to go past the past and be available, responsibility,
embarrassment, tension, despondency, misfortune,
and misuse.

These are the variables that outline the human
condition. The extraordinary news is that we're
creating past this as an animal groups. Living
according to the viewpoint of the miserable, little,
unreliable self is at this point not our only choice.
Another elective is worked inside us- - we're
planned for one more viewpoint on life in which we
are blessed with full comprehension of our own
worth. At the present time, you have the open door
to be a more joyful, more effective variant of
yourself. It's who you genuinely are. Codes for
Energy will assist you with opening it. They are a

framework, a lifestyle, made out of seven
fundamentals, that can assist you with understanding
your fullest
potential. As you investigate every one, you'll
gain proficiency with its importance.

At the point when you see life according to the viewpoint in all actuality by codes for energy, your life becomes deliberate, and, considerably more than that, it becomes fulfilling, An overwhelming inclination of direction and energy pervades each snapshot of your day. You gain areas of strength for of mindfulness, certainty, and association
to the remainder of the world. Feeling self esteem and self-esteem turns into your super durable internal condition. Each venture turns into an outright exhilarating venture in which you are the essential specialist of creation. Intentionally making the things you love turns into a piece of your job as the designer of your life. Life becomes astonishing, loaded up with amazement, surprise, and trust.

Chapter 2

What Codes for Energy Offer

Codes for energy are a bunch of rules that
assist you with creating your own Quantum Flip
-moving from vulnerability, anxiety,
sleepiness, and bothering to strengthening,
satisfaction, concentrate, prosperity, and
innovativeness.
By restoring an ordinary progression of energy
in your body, you change your character
from Protective Personality to Soulful Self.
The Protective Personality is a trepidation based,
endurance centered character that trusts we
are the issue; it is an obliged and excruciating
character. Then again, the Soulful Self
is our certifiable, limitless pith as profound
creatures; the model of ourselves is
faultless, healthy, and complete.
All that inside your life is energy, and
Codes for Energy offer you the abilities to
experience and perceive this to you, body, and soul.
At the point when you take a gander at life from
this perspective, basically all that you do takes on
another importance. For instance, numerous teens

have used this Codes for Energy to find their position on the planet and have stopped hazardous propensities like substance
misuse, scattered eating, and hurting
themselves in the craving to "want." to fit in or have a place blurs when we view and feel ourselves as pioneers, rather than following the group or contrasting ourselves with others. You'll find a persistence and presence you didn't realize you had, and you'll have the option to assume responsibility for your life as the maker and pioneer you've for a long time needed to be.

Chapter 3

The Five Truths of Energy

Distinguishing as the Soulful Self is a significant part of making the Quantum Flip. To do as such, you should initially perceive that a vivacious reality exists under the account layer of your reality. There are five key bits of insight you ought to be aware to appropriately open your psyche to this more profound reality.

~ The principal truth is that everything in the universe is energy, and it is vibrating at various frequencies. Our considerations and feelings are simply unique vibrational frequencies, and, surprisingly, our actual structure is just packed energy. We are one bound together arrangement of energies.

~ The subsequent truth is that your life mirrors your energy. The more scattered your energy, the more disturbed, befuddling, and difficult your life will be. The more incorporated or bound together your energy, the more in control, calm, and euphoric you will be.

~ The third truth is that you're the maker
of your own life. We as a whole can
deal with the energy moving through our
framework and make it more bound together. We as
a whole have the capacity to unwittingly either bring
together or scatter our energy with the food varieties
we eat, the contemplations we think, the manner in
which we treat others, what's more, the connections
we have.

~ The fourth truth is that your life and your
creation are continuously growing. The universe
is growing constantly, and everything in
our lives is a part of that development.
All that happens in your life serves that
development and is consequently great.

~ The fifth truth is that your life object is to
completely understand and recognize your
organization furthermore, creatorship. At the point
when you come into your genuine nature as the
Soulful Self, you quit taking things by and by. You
never again develop the energy obstructions that
keep you caught, or believe yourself to be anything
short of a powerful maker.

Chapter 4

Mental Shifts Towards Codes for Energy

The Codes for Energy are a totally new
technique for mending. Our general public has
frequently moved toward prosperity from an
external perspective in.

We should modify this in the event that we are to ive
the existence we want or, all the more essentially, in
the event that we are to satisfy our fate as genuine
makers. To get the most
out of Codes for Energy, we should make three
mental changes in our view of wellbeing,
recuperating, and personality.

Regardless, what wounds or mends us does
not start just from the rest of the world.

~ We should forsake the idea that as it were
infections, microorganisms, and different organisms
make us "sick," while prescription and medical
procedure make us "solid." Genuine mending and
completeness should rise out of inside, since they
begin in our energy field.

~ Second, we're something beyond people.

At the point when we seek after customary otherworldliness, we will more often than not see ourselves as essentially people in journey of a God or Spirit to save us from our issue. Howbeit, the truth is that we are what we want. We are energy creatures, and since all that in the universe is interrelated, we are unified with the Source, the divine energy. We have our underlying foundations in Heaven, what's more, our definitive objective is to epitomize totally our heavenly Self here on Earth.
~ Lastly, nothing bad can really be said about your life. There are no hardships to tackle, and no obstacles to win. At the point when we do the Quantum Flip, we understand that there was nothing off-base since all that occurs in our lives is for our definitive advantage. It's all in our advantage, and it generally has been.

Chapter 5

The Seven Codes for Energy

There are seven Codes for Energy that initiate the important wiring or hardware inside you to permit you to live as your Soulful Self. The Codes give a complete system for revising lopsided characteristics, arousing to your inward significance, and, in particular, partaking in a superb life. They'll educate you step by step instructions to embrace the truth of what your identity is furthermore, fabricate a daily existence you'll truly cherish. Whether you're new to using energy as medication or a carefully prepared specialist, these leap forward systems give bits of knowledge and techniques that will transform you and the lives of others. Each Code compares to one of the seven chakras, which are the focuses of energy in our bbody.

1. The Anchoring Code. It relates to the Root chakra, at the foundation of the spine. The vast majority of us exist and recognize ourselves as our

mind, imagining that is everything to us. As an outcome, we endeavor to reason our direction
to a superior presence. Nonetheless, the crude energy flowing through the body uncovers a completely different truth about our hidden substance.

We might change our concentration from the outward world to the fiery center that is our real
pith, thus distinguish as that embodiment
the Soulful Self-by concentrating
internal to the body and laying out our
awareness there. The most ideal way to moor
your energy is through rehearses that raise
your familiarity with your own body, for example,
yoga, and the best yoga models for mooring
are the seat, the pyramid, and the tree.

2. The Feeling Code. It
relates to the Sacral chakra, just underneath
the navel. At the point when we are encountering
grinding over the course of our lives, we have three
responses: mental, close to home, and physical. The
Feeling Code says we ought to divert our feelings
into actual sentiments, to more readily manage them

what's more, not let them control our psyches. We can do this by partner a feeling we feel tothe tense sensation it triggers in a piece of our
body, and unclenching that strain to give up
of the inclination. We presently start to initiate our tactile sensory system and show it what it
may feel subsequent to mooring our energy in the body. As we identify and feel energy changes
inside our bodies, we start a discussion
between our genuine self, which is our spirit,
also, our mind. This furnishes us with a
progressive new methodof understanding
also, responding to what happens in our lives while additionally reinforcing our Soulful Self.

3. The Clearing code.
It compares to the Solar Plexus chakra,
at the foundation of the sternum. The majority of us have turned down correspondence between the cognizant and subliminal districts of our
minds because of close to home abundance during huge life altering situations. This implies that we can't accomplish force in life in light of the fact that unsettled worries that exist beyond
our awareness are keeping us down.

As per the Clearing Code, all together to build a day to day existence you love, you initially should acknowledge life all things considered. Then, at that point, you should find approaches to
open the entryway between your cognizant and subliminal personalities so you might adjust
your energy design and communicate the message that those undesirable past life encounters
have been settled, acknowledged, and mended. These ways incorporate high level relaxing strategies, for example, the Morter March and mPower Step, which require a great deal of examination, considering, and practice, yet merit the exertion.

4. The Heart Code. It relates to
the Heart chakra, in the focal point of the chest. The energy we see as adoration is the center energy of the Soulful Self. This energy is our real quintessence and the best vibration we
can feel in actual structure. It's likewise an all inclusive dissolvable, fit for dissolving all obstructions what's more, mending all injuries. As indicated by the Heart Code, we can intentionally create this amazing vibration inside ourselves.

5. The Breath Code.
It relates to the focal point of the chest,
underneath the bosom bone. To show is to
bring something into actual reality. Our breathing is
the greatest tool we have for showing energy in
actual structure. Life
itself, as per the Breath Code, infers
from the breath's energy, essentialness, and life
force. We lessen the Protective Personality
at the point when we inhale our crucial energy into
our enthusiastic densitiesthe regions where we feel
stuck-and invigorate and breathe life into the Soulful
Self when we inhale into the focal point of the
body. There are many breathing procedures,
counting an alternate procedure for each of
the seven chakras, that can assist you with relaxing
energy into your body.

6. The Chemistry Code. It
relates to the Third Eve chakra, in the focal point of
the temple. We're more utilized
to responding to our outer environmental factors
than proactively making the existence we need
from inside. Our ninds and bodies are in
endurance mode, bringing about the pressure based

instinctive reaction. The Chemistry Code
shows us how to rapidly and effectively
convert our physiology from "compromised"
to "safe," permitting our progress from the
Defensive Personality to the Soulful Self. It
shows us how to develop an ideal physical
climate or "home" for extending the
Profound Self's presence. The principal way is
through the food we devour. The body
requires a sound cell climate,
which is accomplished by consuming more
soluble than corrosive food varieties.Probably we
don't,the body will utilize its soluble stores to
balance the destructive corrosive buildup,
forestalling it from going through the
gastrointestinal system what's more, consuming the
kidney and colon tissues, setting off cell breakdown.
If these stores are drained, the body will be in a
debilitated state, not good for the Soulful Self.

7.   The Soul Code. It relates to the Crown
chakra, at the highest point of the head. We distance
ourselves from everything when we distinguish
with the brain: from one another, from the
climate, our own energy-our real,

otherworldly. Howbeit, our structure is
planned for us to feel that connectedness and
unity. The Spirit Code centers around calming
the reasoning brain and being completely present,
with the goal that we may effectively perceive the
heartfelt signals that are constantly ascending
through our bodies and follow up on them with no
trepidation or dithering. There are numerous ways of
putting this into work on, including contemplation,
applying breathing methods while strolling in
nature, also, yoga stances like the cadaver, the
bunny, also, the headstand. Our definitive goal
is to arrive at a place where psyche and soul
cooperate so intently and consistently that they
combine and bring together.

Chapter 6

What Exercises Offer

One of the present significant wellbeing concerns is that sitting for broadened timeframes is awful for our purposes, and along these lines we ought to take ordinary parts from sitting. From certain perspectives specialists, we ought to represent eight minutes also, stroll around for two minutes for each half hour we sit. It's really smart to rehearse some yoga practices during your breaks from sitting.

Yoga has an essentially unique effect than simply getting up and extending. Yoga positions the body in holy mathematical structures that empower higher-recurrence vibrations to flow through it normally, taking advantage of the Soulful Self-which is our definitive objective with least exertion. You might rehearse one position for one chakra on each break, pointing to cover every one of the seven chakras day to day, or you could make a concise output on each break to recognize which chakra needs consideration at the time and select a posture for that.

Breathing activities are another compelling way
to use your sitting break. The Fern Frond
Breath is one that you can rehearse like clockwork
you escape a seat: while breathing out, twist
yourself forward as you get ready to stand, and
then, at that point, while breathing in, spread out
your spine as you tenderly ascent up to a full
position.

At the point when we do works out, we deliberately
infer things that inspire the sense
of appreciation and appreciation. We show
appreciation to emulate the vibrational
frequencies of the Soulful Selfjoy, love,
appreciation, and presence. Each occasion or
second is an opportunity to foster the hardware
that will permit us to mend, extend, and advance
-at the end of the day, to stir as the Soulful
Self.

Chapter 7

Life as the Soulful Self

At the point when we relate to the Soulful Self, we know with amazing conviction that our inward world is the genuine world and the rest of the world is just a projection. Thus, that's what we know "we have this" regardless of what happens. The scientific psyche retreats into the setting, no longer overthinking but instead recognizing that we are the substance we can see, and serving as opposed to engaging our evolvement. Pretty much nothing remains to be finished aside from be who we really are.

Our thoughts are lined up with the more prominent good,and we're ready to see it in all things, We have almost certainly that everything is helping us out -as well as every other person's - and that no matter what, it will generally end up as something good by and by.

Subsequently, love works out easily. There is no dismissal or judgment, just unrestricted acknowledgment and empathy that is secured also, interconnected.

We have confidence in our longings since we know

they are separated through adoration. We are no
longer reluctant to stand up or realize our
dreams, and we take strong and sympathetic
activity. We accept we are great, so we trust
our desires and acts without reservation.
Individuals start to detect and feel areas of strength
for a presence around us when we embrace our
enthusiasm, dreams, and power, and they need
to get closer. Consequently, we pass the reality of
the Profound Self onto them, making a developing
local area of individuals who exist as their valid
selves, and exist and love uninhibitedly.

About the Author

MELVIS MICHAEL is a pharmacist by profession. She's a researcher as well as a writer. She writes on health related topics as well as other fields. Some of her books include ," why women can't sleep;women's new mental implosion" and " The Fasting path".